WOKING
TO
ALTON

Vic Mitchell and Keith Smith

Cover picture: Although the Meon Valley lost its passenger trains in February 1955, a freight service to Farringdon was maintained until August 1968. A typical train is seen in platform 1 at Alton on 9th August 1965, hauled by class Q1 no. 33020, the grimy numbers of which had been highlighted in chalk to the original configuration.
(T. Wright)

Design – Deborah Goodridge

First published October 1988

ISBN 0 906520 59 2

© Middleton Press, 1988

Typeset by CitySet - Bosham 573270

Published by Middleton Press
        Easebourne Lane
        Midhurst, West Sussex
        GU29 9AZ
        ☎ (073 081) 3169

Printed & bound by Biddles Ltd,
        Guildford and Kings Lynn

CONTENTS

ACKNOWLEDGEMENTS

In addition to the photographers mentioned in the captions, we are grateful for the help received from D. Fereday Glenn, J. Fairman, L. James, R. Randell, E. Staff, N. Stanyon and our wives. We also thank D. Wallis and Mrs. M. Mason for use of photographs taken by the late E. Wallis. G. Croughton and N. Langridge have kindly loaned tickets from their collections.

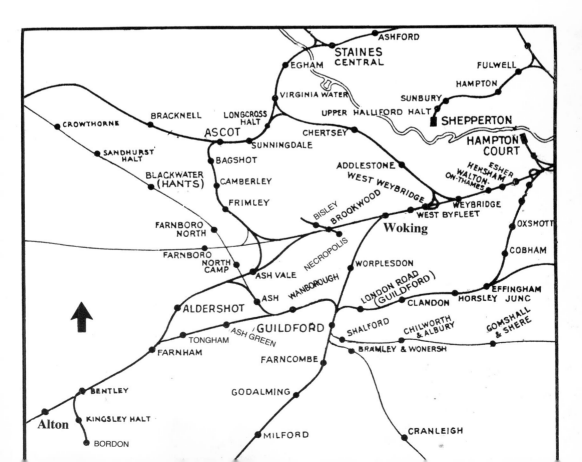

HISTORICAL BACKGROUND

The London & Southampton Railway Company's main line was opened in the Woking area in 1838 and a branch from it to Guildford was completed in 1845, by which time the title "London & South Western Railway" had been adopted.

In the summer of 1849, the SER-operated Reigate to Guildford line was extended to Reading, using part of the LSWR's Guildford to Farnham branch, which was completed on 8th October 1849. This branch was extended from Farnham to Alton on 28th July 1852.

In 1854, work started on the establishment of extensive military camps in the vicinity of the small village of Aldershot. It did not receive a station until 2nd May 1870, when the direct line to London via Ash Vale came into use. The connection to Camberley was opened on 2nd June 1879, while the spur to

the SER, north of Ash, was opened a month earlier.

The branch from Brookwood to the Necropolis Cemetery was opened on 13th November 1854 and closed in 1941 and that from Brookwood to Bisley came into use on 14th July 1890, traffic ceasing on the same day in 1952. The Bentley – Bordon branch was in use for passengers from 11th December 1905 until 16th September 1957, but goods services were maintained until 4th April 1966.

Some electric trains commenced to Farnham on 3rd January 1937, the full service to Alton starting on 4th July 1937. Tongham was not included in the scheme and it lost its passenger service at that time. The three branches, mentioned above, were also outside the electrification programme.

GEOGRAPHICAL SETTING

The first half of the route traverses the extensive infertile sandy soils, long-used as common land and more recently taken over by golf clubs, cemeteries and the army. The line reaches a summit on Pirbright Common and descends into the upper part of the Blackwater Valley. It is in this flat area around Aldershot that the northern part of the River Wey (from Alton) joined the Blackwater River to flow north. In recent geological time, it changed course to join the southern part of the River Wey (from Haslemere) to flow east to Godalming. The

line passes from Surrey into Hampshire at Aldershot North Junction and back into Surrey in the Farnham area.

The railway crosses the chalk linking the North Downs with Salisbury Plain at a geological fault, east of Farnham. This is marked by a gap between the west end of the Hogs Back and the ridge on which Farnham Castle stands.

The line then runs across Gault Clay and proceeds to Alton along the chalk bounded Wey Valley. Two miles west of Farnham, the route passes from Surrey into Hampshire.

All maps are to the scale of 25″ to 1 mile,
unless otherwise stated.

PASSENGER SERVICES

In the 1860's, the Guildford-Alton service usually consisted of five trains each way on weekdays, with two on Sundays. By 1890, there was only one through train to and from Guildford, with the direct service from London via Aldershot comprising seven on weekdays (plus three terminating at Farnham) and two on Sundays. Twenty years later, this had been increased to 14 and 3 respectively. From Guildford, at that time, there were two trains to Alton and seven to Farnham, several of the latter being "Motor Trains".

In 1924, there were 19 weekday departures from Alton towards London but some terminated at Woking. The introduction of a 30-minute interval electric service in 1937 gave 39 trains daily. During World War II, the Sunday service was reduced to hourly and a few trains were withdrawn on weekdays, but restored after the war.

On the 13th May 1985, the first major reduction in service took place. Thereafter, only one train per hour ran to Alton, with an additional one each hour to Farnham on weekdays.

An innovation in the timetable, starting on 16th May 1988, was an hourly service between Aldershot and Reading, via Camberley and Ascot.

Bordon Branch

The initial service of eight weekday and two Sunday trains was increased to fourteen and five by 1910. The frequency changed little in peacetime until 1937, when a weekday hourly interval was maintained to connect with the electric service. Five journeys were made on Sundays. The final timetable showed ten trips daily, at irregular intervals.

1956 timetable, which includes two Woking to Ascot trains that passed under Pirbright Flyover.

LONDON, WOKING, GUILDFORD, ALDERSHOT, FARNHAM, BORDON and ALTON

WOKING

Although the first train from London arrived on 21st May 1838, the town was very slow to develop. The ancient village of Woking was 1½ miles south of the station but the town started to grow north of the railway, the following facts highlighting its progress to maturity – first place of worship (Methodist) 1872; first school 1875; piped water 1883; police station 1886; electricity 1890; gas supply 1892; fire station 1894 and main sewers in 1899.

1. The station was known as "Woking Common" initially, becoming "Woking Junction" from 1845 until 1913. The first station was rebuilt when the Guildford branch opened in 1845 and further rebuilding took place in 1879, when a third track was added. This 1894 photograph shows part of the 1888 rebuild. The lad porter on the right is B.W. West, who retired as chief goods clerk at Woking in 1939. (K. West collection)

2. The station was totally reconstructed in 1937-38 and this picture from 5th January 1937 shows the new signal box and goods shed partially erected. No. 861 *Lord Anson* passes through with the "Atlantic Coast Express" while class M7 no. 30 waits in the down bay with a local train to Ascot. Headboards were not used until after WWII. (J.R.W. Kirkby)

3. An up bay was also provided and class N15 no. 777 *Sir Lamiel* is seen standing in it on 12th May 1947 while acting as a standby engine for a royal train. In 1986, this locomotive was once again hauling special trains on BR, often operating from Marylebone. This platform was eliminated in 1968 to allow for the provision of a long lay-by for buses. (K. Nunn/LCGB)

4. A 1955 view from the down local platform shows the 1937 signal box, which was still in use over 50 years later, and the goods shed, which was demolished in April 1988 to provide more car parking spaces. Conductor rails were provided in 1937, for the Portsmouth and Alton electrifications, and the control room for the area was built near the junction. (D. Cullum)

5. 4VEP unit no. 7702 forms the 10.50 from Alton on 19th November 1983 and awaits the attachment of the four coaches of a stopping train from Bournemouth. It stands at platform 2 which has since been renumbered 1, as the original no. 1 (the up bay) was behind the wall and was seen in picture no. 3. (A. Dasi-Sutton)

6. The Junction Box was one of three at Woking and was built in 1877. It closed in 1937 by which time it had acquired a 100-lever frame. Chief Signalman William West was photographed in 1894. Until 1903, the next box west was Goldsworth Cutting Box, which was abolished with the quadrupling of the tracks. (K. West collection)

7. Class M7 no. 676 departs for Ascot on 29th October 1938 on the down local line. The gap between this and the down main indicates the site of the Junction Box. The Portsmouth line diverges in the background. (H.C. Casserley)

8. With Woking station in the distance, no. D6549 departs west on the local line on 27th August 1966. The yard on the left was used as a marshalling yard until that at Feltham came into use in 1921, and the one in the right distance was used for local goods until 1st June 1970. In 1988, it was receiving a substantial traffic of roadstone. (T. Wright)

9. The tower block of British American Tobacco typifies modern Woking as a commercial centre. This has given rise to a two-way commuter passenger traffic of some magnitude. Another new through traffic is crude oil, seen here on 26th September 1986 in transit from Holybourne (near Alton) to Fawley. The locomotive is Railfreight class 47/3 no. 47363 *Billingham Enterprise*. (C. Wilson)

10. For about 30 years, 2 BILs were provided for most of the Alton services. Nos. 2135 and 2015 approach Woking on 15th July 1966, with the 11.24 service from Alton, and pass the lengthy sidings of the up yard. 7 was the up headcode, 12 being used on down trains. (J.H. Bird)

Maps and other photographs of Woking can be seen in our *Waterloo to Woking, Woking to Portsmouth, Woking to Southampton* and Peter Hay's *Steaming through Surrey.*

BROOKWOOD

11. The up-platform signs reveal the importance of this station, which was opened on 1st June 1864. Details of the branches to both locations are to be found in the following pages. Note that the main lines are devoid of conductor rails – they were not required until the advent of the Bournemouth electrification scheme in 1967. (Lens of Sutton)

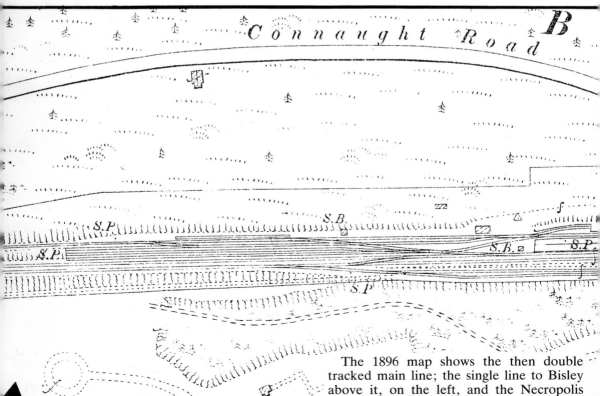

The 1896 map shows the then double tracked main line; the single line to Bisley above it, on the left, and the Necropolis branch, lower right. "Refreshment Room" refers to part of the Necropolis Cemetery's

12. The three signal boxes shown on the 1896 map were replaced by this pneumatic one in 1907. It had 33 "levers" operating 15 points and 18 signals, pneumatically. There were also four automatic air-operated signals to the east. The box closed on 5th June 1966. (Lens of Sutton)

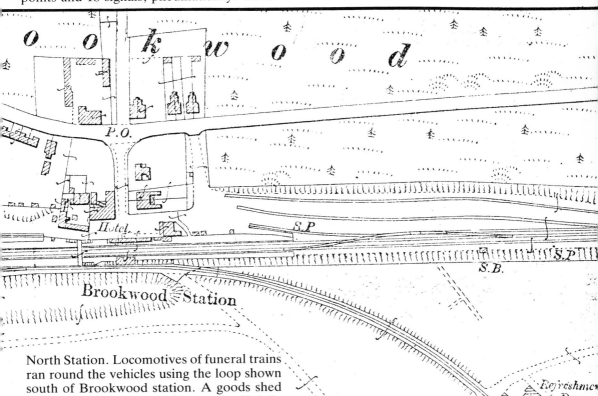

North Station. Locomotives of funeral trains ran round the vehicles using the loop shown south of Brookwood station. A goods shed was added in 1903 and the yard officially closed on 1st May 1961.

13. The grass covered tracks of the Bisley bay were taken out of use in 1965 although the branch closed to passengers in 1952. The down platform, on the right, had been repositioned to the south during the quadrupling of the main line in 1903-04. (Lens of Sutton)

BISLEY BRANCH

ALIGHT ON THE OTHER SIDE

30027

14. The original buildings were replaced in 1890 and extensions made in 1903, a subway giving access to the cemetery and the down platform. The only architectural feature to have been lost is a porch over the main door. When all Network SouthEast lamp posts were being painted blood red, the posts here were tactfully treated with black paint. (C. Hall)

15. The line was opened on 12th July 1890 and the bay platform at Brookwood was separated from the up platform by railings which ran between the lamp post and the signal bridge support, seen on the right of this July 1952 photograph. Access was through the gates by the barrow. (D. Clayton)

> **Additional maps and views of this station are included in the *Woking to Southampton* album.**

←

16. Push-pull operation became common practice in the 1930s and continued until closure. A class D1 0-4-2T propels set no. 23 into Brookwood on 4th July 1939. The hand operated points were clipped and padlocked during the passenger carrying week. (J.R.W. Kirkby)

←

17. The route ran parallel to the main line for ½ mile and then curved away north and crossed the Basingstoke Canal on the major civil engineering feature of the branch. The canal is fully described in *Surrey Waterways* (Middleton Press) and is slowly being restored to working order. (D. Cullum collection)

18. Set no. 734 returns from Bisley on 12th July 1952, descending the 1 in 50 and 1 in 89 gradient onto the canal bridge. The canal in this area last saw commercial traffic in 1921 and was reopened for pleasure purposes in 1985. (D. Cullum)

The National Rifle Association was forced to vacate its premises on Wimbledon Common in 1888 and the LSWR encouraged it to move to another site on their system. Bisley Common was chosen and army personnel constructed the branch line under a Tramways Act. Trains were provided and operated by the LSWR and, in peacetime, were only run regularly for a week annually, during the July meeting.

19. The road from Pirbright Bridge to Bisley Camp passed over the line on Cowshot Bridge, Cowshot Farm and Cowshot Manor being east of the track. Class M7 no. 30027 proceeds north on 12th July 1952. (Pamlin Prints)

21. The driver's compartment is crowded, as he eases his train round the final curve into Bisley on 19th July 1952. A similar speed restriction board was situated by the buffers of the long sidings at Brookwood. The station was still standing in 1988 and had a sleeping car at the platform! (J.J. Smith)

20. 300 yards north of the road bridge, the line crossed a track to Cowshot Common. Much of the route passed through dense woodland which was surrounded by open heathland on which the ranges were situated. (D. Cullum)

22. A pre-WWI photograph shows a locomotive in the process of running round its
train, also the hut-like terminal buildings
with nameboard and finials on the roof.

Assorted sun hats process past the advertise-
ments for the official NRA optician.
(Lens of Sutton)

23. For the last meeting before WWII,
Guildford shed provided ex-LBSCR 0-4-2T
no. 2220 for the service. It was photographed
on 15th July 1939. During both world wars,

Bisley Camp was used for small arms training
and numerous extra trains were run.
(J.R.W. Kirkby)

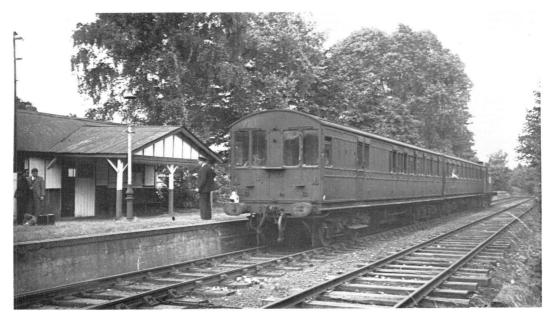

24. When photographed on 12th July 1947, the appearance of the station had been improved by the addition of a canopy. Class M7 no. 128 and push-pull set no. 721 were in use. (S.C. Nash)

25. Viewed a few minutes later, no. 128 had been artistically adorned with the train's unofficial name – "Bisley Bullett". The loop line was still in situ but only used as a siding. Note the odd length sleepers and flat bottom rail. (S.C. Nash)

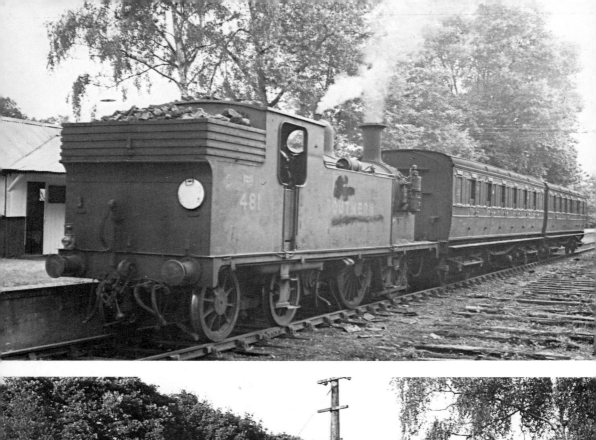

26. The locomotive was at the west of the train when seen on 7th July 1950, no. 481 being one of a number of class M7s used on the branch. Under its bogie, the rail section becomes larger towards the buffer stops, a once common practice. The loop rails have been lifted. (S.C. Nash)

27. This is the scene on the last day of public service – 19th July 1952. In earlier years, some through trains were run from Waterloo for Territorial Army camps, the timetable allowing 67 to 76 minutes for the journey. (J.J. Smith)

28. In the summer of 1948, extra trains had been run in connection with part of the Olympic Games, which were held in Britain that year. The final special train is seen on 23rd November 1952, headed by class M7 no. 30027, a familiar engine on the branch. The lattice gates on the ex-LSWR coaches were less familiar. (P. Hay)

The 1920 map at 6″ to 1 mile shows the extension of the Bisley branch, which was opened in March 1917 to serve the barracks at Pirbright, Deepcut and Blackdown. The line climbed at 1 in 55 from Deepcut to Blackdown and was built entirely on WD land. It was operated by military locomotives from the nearby Woolmer Instructional Military Railway, described in our *Branch Lines to Longmoor*. The engine shed is shown lower left, as is the main line to Basingstoke. The Alton line is at the bottom of this page, the up line passing over a flyover at Pirbright Junction. The Basingstoke Canal can be seen running roughly parallel to the main line, the builders of which were required to erect a wall to prevent trains frightening the bargees' horses. The Bisley-Brookwood line can be found on a map to the same scale, opposite picture 10 in the *Woking to Southampton* album. The Bisley-Blackdown section was closed in 1921 but relaid again in WWII, as far as Pirbright Camp.

29. Deepcut Camp station was gigantic when compared with Bisley, and was capable of taking full length troop trains. WIMR 0-6-2T *Sir John French* is seen with a train from Bisley. Note the absence of platform ramps, required on public railways. (Lens of Sutton)

30. This is booking hall no. 1 at Deepcut Camp station, the ticket office window being in the end wall, between the two men. W.H. Smith & Son unfortunately were displaying a German abbreviation. (Lens of Sutton)

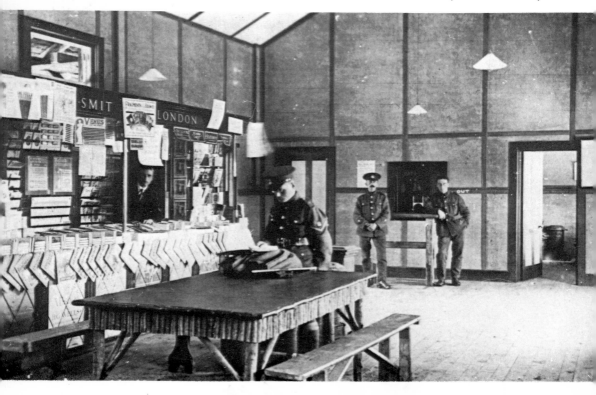

NECROPOLIS CEMETERY

In 1850, further burials in London were prohibited, as most cemeteries were then full. In 1852, the London Necropolis and Mausoleum Company (Necropolis Co. hereinafter) was formed and it purchased the 2268 acres of Woking Common. Only 400 acres were eventually used for the cemetery and Woking gradually developed in an unplanned manner on much of the remaining land. The cemetery was consecrated and officially opened on 7th November 1854, a ¾ mile-long branch into it being provided for trains from London. The Necropolis Co. had its own station in Westminster Bridge Road (see photograph no. 2 in *Waterloo to Windsor* and no. 21 in *Waterloo to Woking*). A daily train was run until 1900 (weekdays only thereafter), the company initially providing the special hearse vans for the coffins and the LSWR providing locomotive, coaches and crew.

31. North Station was the first one on the branch and was close to the Non-conformist Chapel and the Roman Catholic Chapel. The two chalet-style buildings contained mourners' rooms and flanked a courtyard, which was bounded by refreshment rooms. (Lens of Sutton)

32. The timber buildings were intended as temporary structures but North Station (viewed from the east) stood for over 100 years. The dip in the platform edge is reputed to have facilitated the unloading of coffins.

The sleepers were covered by ballast and were a cause of concern for the SR who feared for the safety of their rolling stock. (Lens of Sutton)

33. South Station was the terminus and was situated in the Anglican part of the cemetery. Between the stations a trailing siding was added on the east side of the line, in about 1905, to serve the stone mason's yard. This is the view towards the buffers, in 1930. (H.C. Casserley)

34. Class M7 no. 244 stands at South Station on 30th May 1930, having propelled its train the full length of the line. Funeral trains ceased to run in May 1941 when the 3rd class part of the London terminus was destroyed by enemy bombs. The branch line track was removed in 1953. (H.C. Casserley)

35. Pirbright Junction flyover was completed in 1902, so that the level junction could be eliminated prior to the quadrupling. A new signal box was opened in 1904 but was closed in 1931. This photograph, from 18th April 1963, shows the new concrete joists, which replaced the original steel spans. London to Southampton trains were sometimes diverted at Pirbright Junction to run via Aldershot and Alton to Winchester Junction, particularly during the electrification of the main line. (British Rail)

36. Foxhills Tunnel is 418 yds long and midway on the two-mile journey across the almost uninhabited Pirbright Common. East of the tunnel, a signal box acted as a block post on the up line only, from 1936 to 1960. (British Rail)

ASH VALE

37. Opened as "North Camp and Ash Vale" on 2nd May 1870, the name was changed to "Ash Vale" on 30th March 1924. The nameboard was more informative, when photographed with a push-pull set enveloped in its own steam on a misty day in February 1936. (H.C. Casserley)

38. The Camberley line passes behind the signal box on the left and the Woking line runs under the bridge in the distance. Prior to WWII, this bridge gave access to the depot of the Corps of Military Police. The photograph was taken in 1966 – the crossover was removed twelve years later. (D. Cullum)

39. Opposite the signal box is a tablet catcher for the single line to Frimley Junction which commences to the right of this 1955 picture. A 4COR unit stands in the station, this type of stock being used on some peak hour Farnham services. (D. Cullum)

The 1931 survey shows pleasure boat houses on the bank of the Basingstoke Canal. Commercial barges were also built here for many years – see pictures 39 to 43 in *Surrey* *Waterways*. Little Mytchett Flash was a hollow in the land which became flooded when the canal was opened in 1794.

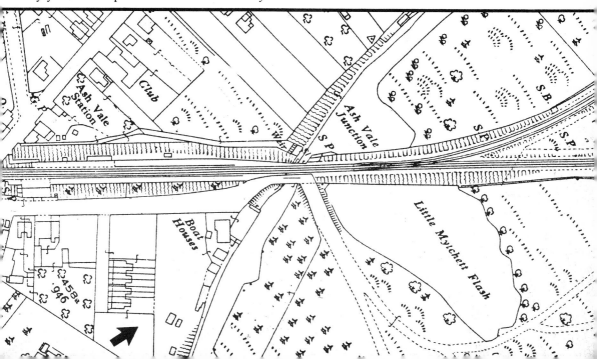

40. The main building was on the down side and had architectural features similar to those of Aldershot station, both having been built for the opening of the line. This 1966 view shows that the RAMC were occupying the former MP depot by then. (D. Cullum)

41. A 1969 photograph of the down platform on 19th May shows the 11.58 Waterloo to Guildford restarting. 2HAL no. 2626 would reverse at Aldershot, having travelled via Staines and Camberley. (J.H. Bird)

42. 4 VEPs began to displace the original wooden bodied stock on the route in 1967. This example heads the 09.34 Alton to Waterloo on 22nd June 1988, by then reclassified as class 423. (J. Scrace)

43. The south facade, seen on the same day, requires less maintenance than its predecessor, which had to be demolished owing to subsidence. The new station was completed in 1972. (J. Scrace)

ALDERSHOT

Since 1248 the village has been chronicled with no less than nineteen different spellings but it was not until 1854 that it assumed any importance. Its population of about 900 increased rapidly, as the army moved into the district at that time. In 1860, construction of the first permanent barracks commenced, with South Camp being laid out between the village and the Basingstoke Canal. North Camp was situated some distance north of the canal. The town achieved borough status in 1922 and now has *nine* museums covering various aspects of military life.

←

The 1912 survey at 6″ to 1 mile shows the Basingstoke Canal passing under the railway, Aldershot North Junction being just off the top of the page. The "Government Sidings" diverge on the west side of the line – these are shown in more detail on the following pages. The main line climbs at 1 in 120 from these sidings, through the 76 yd long Aldershot Tunnel, to the station. The gasworks on the right were rail connected at Tongham – see picture no. 65. From 1879, SER trains ran to Aldershot from Ash via Aldershot Junction (North and South). Most started at Ash but there were some through services to London Bridge or Cannon Street, via Redhill.

The first Government Siding was brought into use in 1890 and is seen diverging from the main line, lower left, on this 1931 map. The signal box was replaced by a ground frame on 23rd August 1970. The line no longer crosses the road near Ash Lock (top right) and, in 1988, terminated in two sidings retained by the Railway Detachment, Royal Corps of Transport, for vehicle movement. The circles are gasholders and the dots and dashes, on the main line, represent the ward boundary.

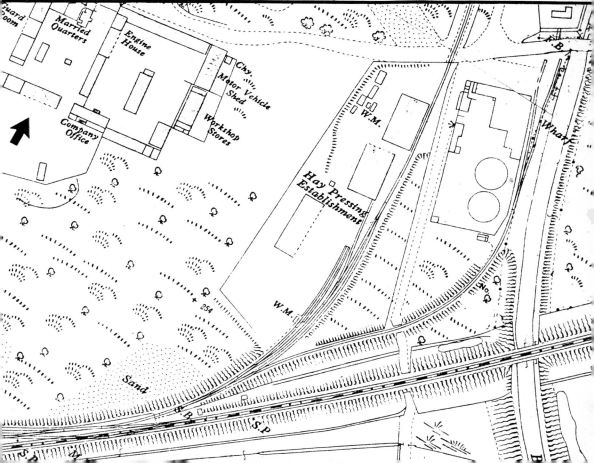

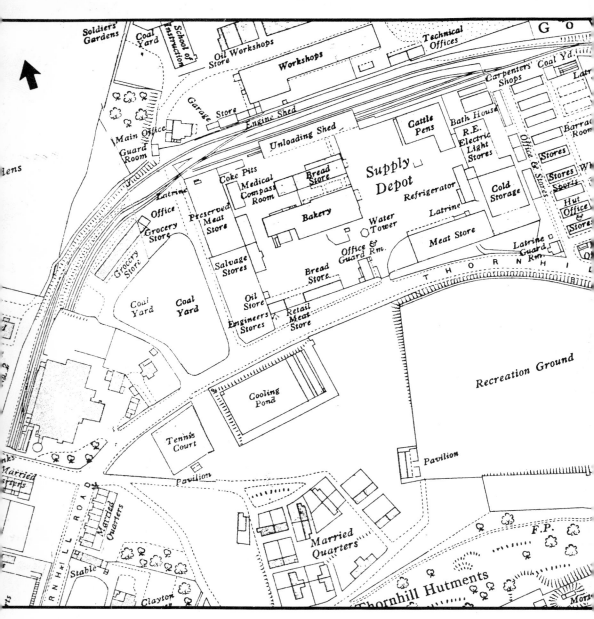

The north siding terminated at the electric power station (left) but coal was not the main traffic – the names on this 1931 map indicate that food often predominated.

The 1931 edition reveals that the south sidings were used for non-edible stores. In 1988, the lines no longer crossed the road (at the top) but terminated in a loop near the REME Depot.

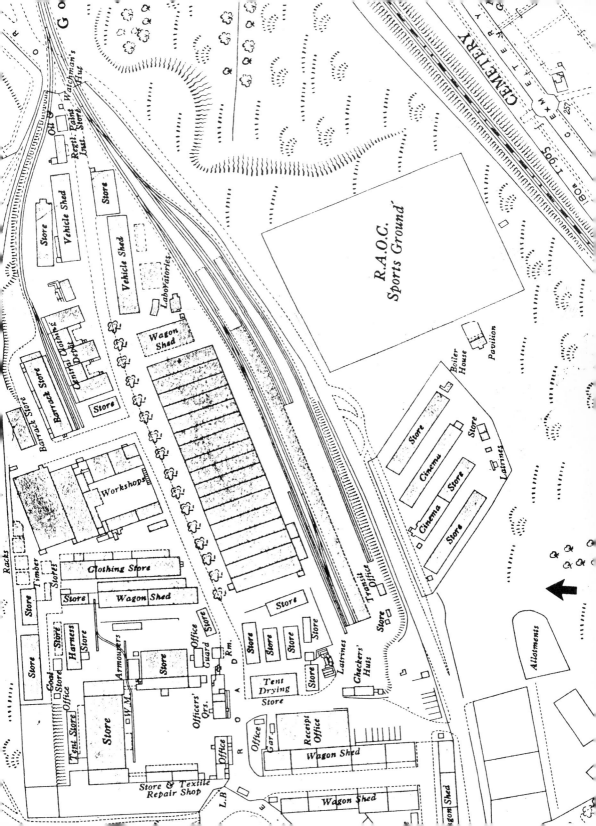

44. The south sidings ended with three platforms, two of which were covered. HM King George V is seen on the right, between the two LSWR cattle wagons, on 20th May 1914. (Aldershot Military Historical Trust)

45. The platforms were once the scene of great activity with troop train movements or special trains for visitors to the Aldershot Tattoo. This is the northward view in January 1985, shortly before the site was cleared. (Aldershot Military Historical Trust)

46. A pre-WWI view of the north side of the station includes the end of the SER sidings on the left. From 1899, the SER and "Chatham" lines (LCDR) were operated by a joint managing committee as the SECR. (Lens of Sutton)

47. Maybe a royal visit has prompted the bunting to be unfurled above the usual enamelled signs for ales and stouts. This is the view north from the down platform. (Lens of Sutton)

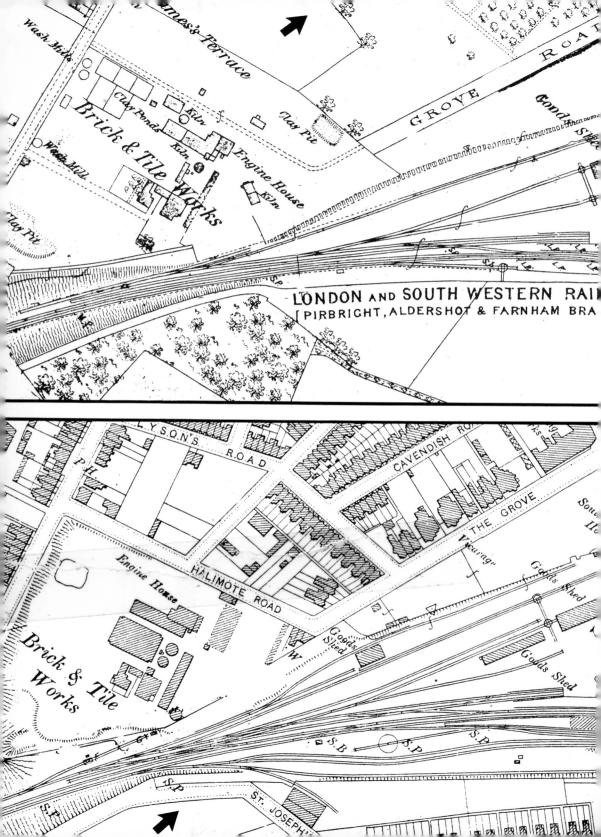

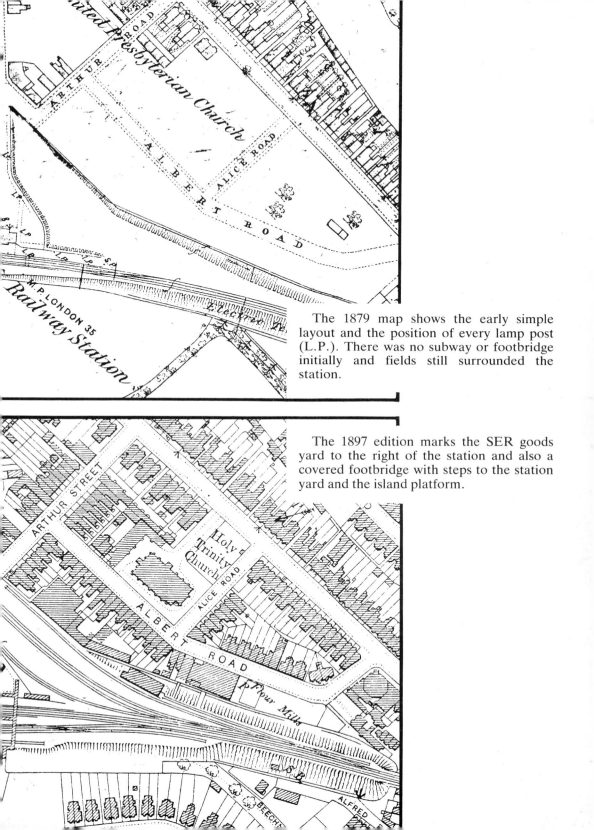

The 1879 map shows the early simple layout and the position of every lamp post (L.P.). There was no subway or footbridge initially and fields still surrounded the station.

The 1897 edition marks the SER goods yard to the right of the station and also a covered footbridge with steps to the station yard and the island platform.

48. The northward panorama from the five-arched bridge that carries Church Lane East over the line contains both LSWR yards and a train departing for Farnham.
(Lens of Sutton)

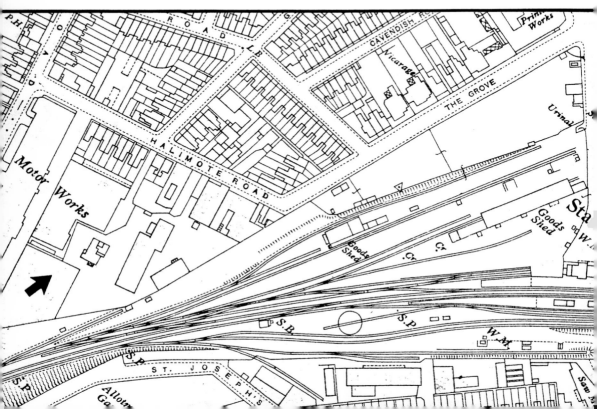

49. The headcode indicates Waterloo to Southampton Terminus via Alton. Until 1937, most London trains ran to and from Southampton or Gosport. Class X6 4-4-0 no. E592 was built in 1892 and withdrawn in 1936. (Lens of Sutton)

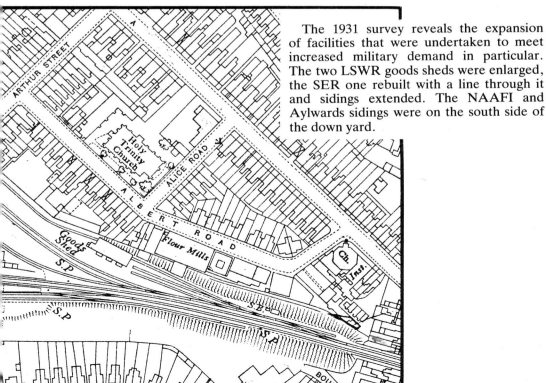

The 1931 survey reveals the expansion of facilities that were undertaken to meet increased military demand in particular. The two LSWR goods sheds were enlarged, the SER one rebuilt with a line through it and sidings extended. The NAAFI and Aylwards sidings were on the south side of the down yard.

50. Class M7 no. 111 is seen waiting to propel its coaches back to the bay platform at Ash at 12.39 pm on 29th November 1938. This shuttle service connected with the Guildford-Reading trains and was discontinued when the Aldershot-Guildford route was electrified on 2nd July 1939. (J.R.W. Kirkby)

51. Another class M7 was to be found shunting the western yard on 21st March 1959, with a container on a flat wagon next to the engine. The buses belonged to the Aldershot & District Traction Co. who were faithful, for decades, to the Guildford-based vehicle manufacturer – Dennis. (T. Wright)

52. Electro-diesel no. E6044, with shoes retracted, is working in multiple with "Crompton" no. D6509 on 11th February 1967, with a freight service to Feltham Marshalling Yard. One of the 10 ton capacity goods cranes is partially visible. (R.E. Ruffell)

53. 2HAL unit no. 2653 was on the solitary electrified siding on 29th October 1968 when it was in collision with coal wagons on the adjacent siding. 2BIL no. 2011 passes the 1896 West Box, by then designated 'B Box'. Only the electrified siding and one for the engineers remained in 1988. (R.E. Ruffell)

54. Looking towards Farnham in 1970, we see the 50ft. diameter turntable, with its connection to the loop line and 'B Box', which was closed on 3rd April 1977. Five-arch bridge is in the distance. (J. Scrace)

55. Sliding-door stock was not introduced on the Southern Region until late in 1979 but, on 18th July 1972, experimental units nos. 2001 and 4002 appeared at Aldershot on trial. Note the Scharfenberg coupling, widely used in mainland Europe. (R.E. Ruffell)

56. Looking at the east end of the station in January 1973, the second locomotive water tank and the public footbridge are in view. A subway was provided for passengers in about 1897. The yard on the right was used as a coal concentration depot from 6th January 1969 but goods facilities were withdrawn entirely on 6th October 1975. (R.E. Ruffell)

57. The fine symmetrical frontage was renovated in 1988, the year in which the proprietors of the bookstall dropped "& Son". Presumably no posthumous offence occurs, as the son was also W.H. Smith. (C. Hall)

58. This is the London end of the platforms in January 1985 with the portal of Aldershot Tunnel close to the floodlights of Aldershot Football Club. The Former 'A Box' is at the end of the up platform and was still in use in 1988. (J.H. Bird)

59. As the skyline testifies, Aldershot is rapidly becoming a commercial centre, like Woking, as its military importance declines. The former goods yard is often occupied by vans delivering to branches of Boots The Chemist. The train is the "Watercress Belle", composed of the Mid-Hants Railway's dining cars and departed from Woking at 13.25 on 29th May 1988, in connection with the *WOKING 150* celebrations. These commemorated the arrival of the first train there, 150 years earlier. (C. Wilson)

FARNHAM JUNCTION

60. Class L12 no. 30434 rounds the 14 chain curve from Aldershot on 26th September 1953, with the Railway Enthusiasts Club special to Bordon and Longmoor. It is joining the original main line from Guildford which, by then, had been singled and the two miles to Tongham was only used for stock storage. 310 wagons could be stored but gaps had to be left for the two occupation crossings. The sub-station still displays its wartime camouflage paint. (S.C. Nash)

61. The signal box was on the north side of the line, as were two sidings prior to WWII. A ballast pit siding was situated to the west and Patterson's siding branched from the up Aldershot line. (Lens of Sutton)

62. The Tongham line closed on 21st November 1954 and the signal box followed on 5th May 1964. The instrument shelf is about to follow the same trajectory as the front of the box. (Lens of Sutton)

TONGHAM

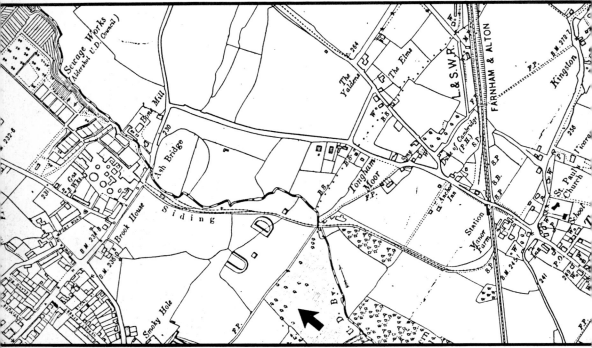

The 1912 map at 6″ to 1 mile has the Guildford to Farnham line running from top to bottom. West of the station, which opened in October 1856, a long siding curves north to Aldershot Gasworks. It crossed Ash Road, near Ash Bridge. The works is seen on the right of the Aldershot 6″ to 1 mile map.

The small village did not become incorporated into the area of military development but its station served South Aldershot until 1870. The little station was very busy, in the early 1860s, handling vast tonnages of materials for the construction of the permanent army camps.

63. The entrance was on the west side of the bridge and a covered staircase led from the booking hall down to the up platform. Open steps were provided to the down platform, adjacent to the factory. (Lens of Sutton)

64. Looking towards Ash Junction and Guildford on 8th March 1938, we see the unusual barrow crossing which runs in the track from the drop in the up platform, before crossing to the ramp of the down platform. After 9th February 1932, all trains used the down line and Tongham signal box was dispensed with. (F.E. Box/NRM)

65. A view from the up platform towards Farnham in July 1947 includes a van in McArthy's siding (the white gates are across it); wagons standing on the former up line (it was used as a siding each side of the station) and the commencement of the gasworks line on the right. (J.H. Aston)

66. Sandwiched by brake vans, class U no. 31614 propels coal wagons through the gates to the gasworks siding on 19th January 1952. The works engine would collect from there. One such engine is to be seen in picture no. 95 in our *Reading to Guildford* album. (D. Cullum)

67. An enthusiasts' railtour visited Tongham on 5th October 1957, hauled by a class M7. By then, the main buildings had been demolished to allow for the erection of a steel footbridge, similar to that at Aldershot. Beyond the rear coach is a short War Department siding. (R.M. Casserley)

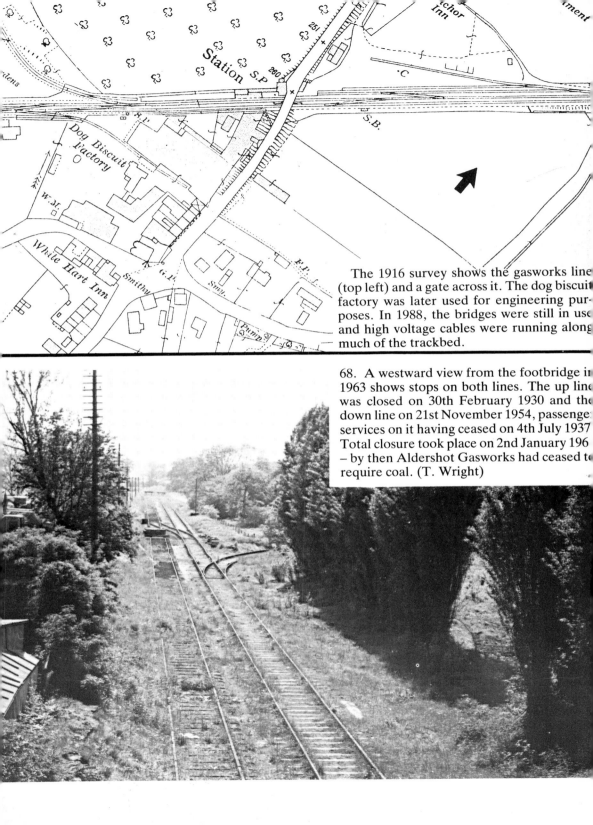

The 1916 survey shows the gasworks line (top left) and a gate across it. The dog biscuit factory was later used for engineering purposes. In 1988, the bridges were still in use and high voltage cables were running along much of the trackbed.

68. A westward view from the footbridge in 1963 shows stops on both lines. The up line was closed on 30th February 1930 and the down line on 21st November 1954, passenger services on it having ceased on 4th July 1937. Total closure took place on 2nd January 196. – by then Aldershot Gasworks had ceased to require coal. (T. Wright)

ASH GREEN

69. The station was opened with the line as "Ash", "Green" being added in 1876, dropped in 1891 and added again in 1895. When staffing ceased and the goods yard closed on 1st December 1926, "Halt" was added. The passenger entrance was down the covered steps, to the left of the building, which still serves as a dwelling. (Lens of Sutton)

70. The bottom of the covered steps can be seen on the disused up platform. As at Tongham, passenger trains between Guildford and Farnham called at the down platform until 4th July 1937. This is the scene in 1952, when only an occasional freight train disturbed the rural peace. (D. Cullum)

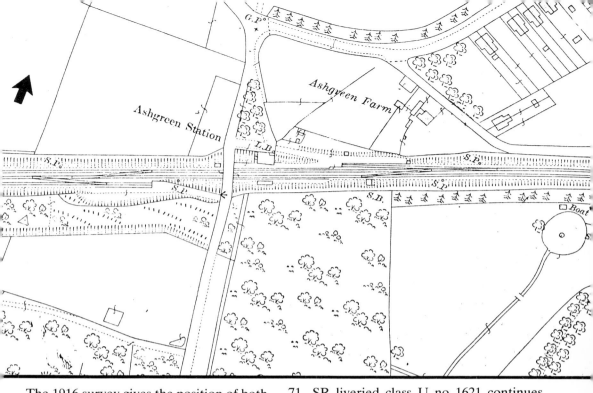

The 1916 survey gives the position of both sidings, both crossovers and the signal box, all of which were taken out of use on 15th May 1927.

71. SR liveried class U no. 1621 continues the climb at 1 in 121 from Wanborough to Ash Green, passing Ash Junction Box, with coal for Aldershot Gasworks. Picture nos. 90 and 91 in *Reading to Guildford* give other views of this junction. (D. Cullum collection)

FARNHAM

72. The station was the terminus of the LSWR branch from Guildford between 8th October 1849 and 28th July 1852. The bridge in the distance linked two fields. This early undated photograph has regrettably been touched up but does pre-date semaphore signals. (Lens of Sutton)

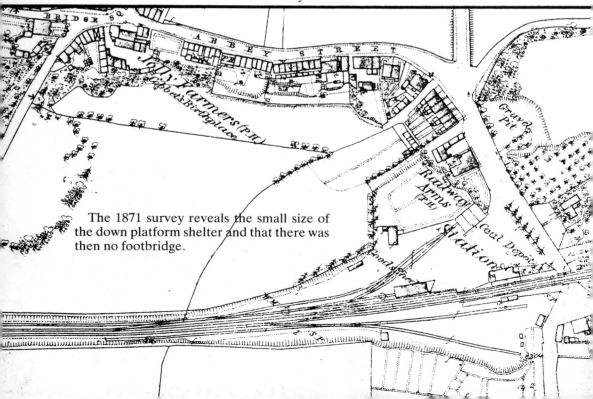

The 1871 survey reveals the small size of the down platform shelter and that there was then no footbridge.

73. The down bay platform, on the right, was taken out of use in 1936 so that the through platform could be extended, prior to electrification. The yard on the right was used mainly for coal traffic. (Lens of Sutton)

The historic town retains many of its Georgian buildings, notably in Castle Street. The red-brick castle stands on high land, north of the town centre, and was the palace of the Bishop of Winchester until 1927 and the Bishop of Guildford until 1956. A more recent role has been as the Centre for International Briefing. The large maltings, in use as such until 1955, have now become well known for varied community functions.

74. In September 1905, the LSWR started a feeder bus service through the villages north of Haslemere, using a 16-seater Thornycroft, two more being added in 1907. In June 1913, this service was taken over by the Aldershot & District Traction Co. and eventually became part of route 19, between Aldershot and Midhurst stations. (Pamlin Prints)

75. Behind the signalman in East Box is the gate wheel for controlling the level crossing which is being traversed by a class 0395 "Jumbo". The box closed on 23rd December 1973, when the gates were replaced by full lifting barriers controlled under CCTV from Farnham West Box. (Lens of Sutton)

76. The covered footbridge is visible in this picture of N class 2-6-0 no. 31816 hauling the 12.25 Woking to Alton parcels service on 11th December, 1965. The Post Office also required many extra trains in the pre-Christmas period. The footbridge is divided by railings, to segregate passengers from the public. (E. Wilmshurst)

The 1934 edition indicates the position of both signal boxes and the full extent of the goods yards. The sidings on the left (lower) were used by Hookstile Minerals and there were also sidings each side of the main line, east of the level crossing, for stock storage.

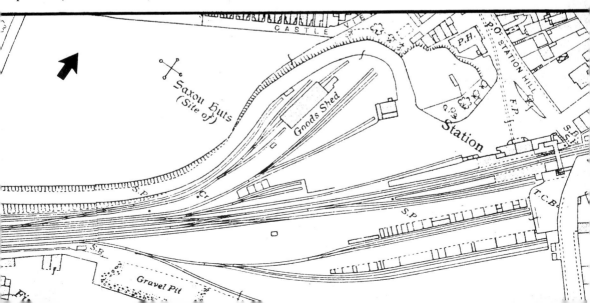

77. The goods yard closed on 4th May 1970 but many of the tracks were still in place when photographed in September 1984. While awaiting transfer to the Mid-Hants Railway, no. 08288 had much of its wiring destroyed by vandals but subsequently became a useful shunter at Ropley. (J.H. Bird)

78. The north facade is shown in 1986, with the wooden parcels office on the left and the windows of the former station master's office on the extreme right. In 1988, new train crew rooms were built, to the right of this picture, and the goods shed was still standing, in use by a plant hire firm. (J.H. Bird)

79. January 1986 presented difficulties for operating staff and for passengers who had left their cars on the site of the former goods yard. 4 VEP no. 7772 is in transit from Selhurst to Farnham Depots and passes the sole surviving signal box which controls the remainder of the route. (J.H. Bird)

The 1871 survey shows the still single line to Alton (doubled on 2nd June 1901) and a small locomotive shed situated close to the main road (top left), west of the present carriage sheds.

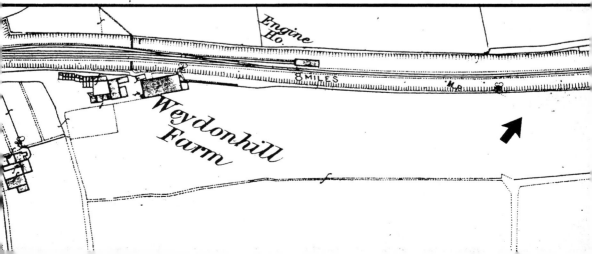

FARNHAM DEPOT

80. The five-road carriage shed was completed in 1937, the local authority at Alton having rejected its presence there, a move which was detrimental to future services to the town. On the left is Weydon Hill siding, which was used for loading gravel until 1968 and was controlled by the ground frame seen beyond the wagons. It was photographed during the 1955 strike.
(D. Cullum collection)

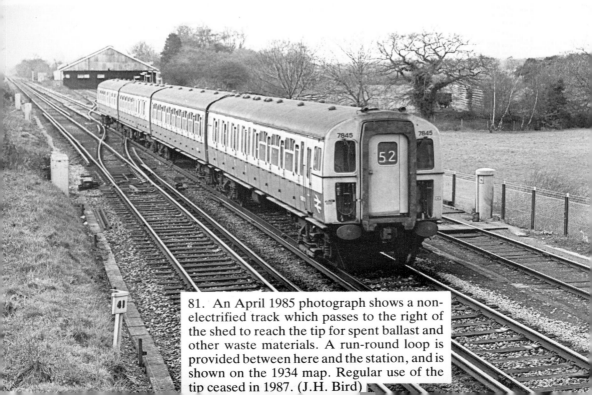

81. An April 1985 photograph shows a non-electrified track which passes to the right of the shed to reach the tip for spent ballast and other waste materials. A run-round loop is provided between here and the station, and is shown on the 1934 map. Regular use of the tip ceased in 1987. (J.H. Bird)

82. Canopies were erected on the platforms prior to the time of the track doubling in 1901. A bay platform, on the right, came into use for the Bordon trains when the branch opened on 11th December 1905. The churns show that the line has reached more fertile land and the tender was for fresh water supply. (Lens of Sutton)

In 1870, the station was a passing place on the single line and was equipped with just one signal. The goods shed was demolished in about 1900.

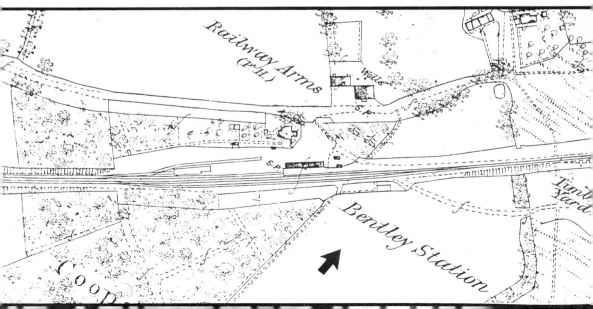

83. Class M7 no. 131 stops with an Alton train on 17th May 1934, the nameboard correctly indicating the legal status of the branch line. The lamps were still oil lit at this time. The pebble-dashed extension was a goods shed. (H.C. Casserley)

The 1910 edition shows two signal boxes. The one on the right had closed in 1905 when the other came into use. The crane (Cr.) was of 5-ton capacity.

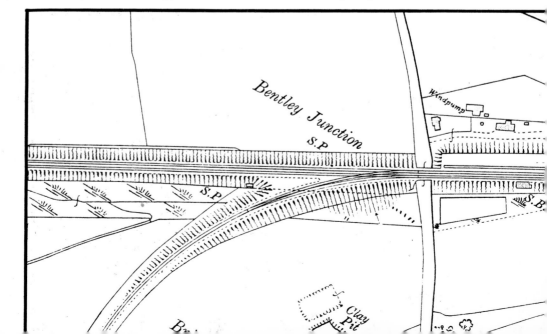

84. A Bordon train departs behind class M7 no. 30056 and runs onto the down main line for the short journey to the junction. Up branch trains similarly used the up main line as, suprisingly, no independent third track was provided. The empty train then had to be shunted over the down line, to reach the bay. (Lens of Sutton)

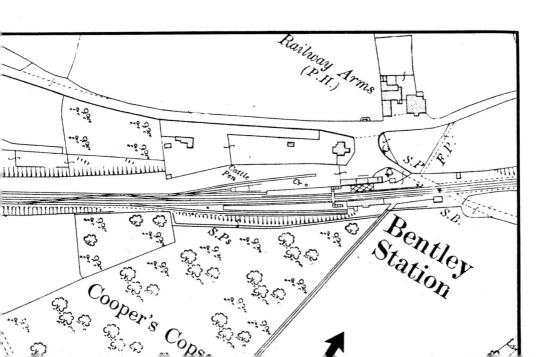

85. The signalman's view east in 1953 shows that uninsulated telephone wires were still in use and that goods wagons were unloaded at the west end of the yard, which closed on 1st June 1964. This was a classical country junction, worthy of a large photograph. (D. Cullum)

86. Only post-WWII photographs show the mid-platform railings, in which there was a gap mid-way. This would have facilitated ticket inspection, particularly when so many soldiers were travelling. Class M7 no. 30027 was on duty on 5th August 1957. (A.E. Bennett)

87. The S15 Commemorative Railtour is about to set forth for Bordon on 16th January 1966. There is ample evidence for the curtailment of steam specials on the Southern, as photographers stand on a running line, close to a live rail, with ice under foot. The train arrived with class S15 no. 30837 piloting. Class U no. 31639 then took the train to Bordon and the two were later reunited at Alton for the climb "over the Alps" to Eastleigh. This was a repeat of the tour operated on the previous Saturday. (R.E. Ruffell)

88. The 15.27 from Waterloo arrives on 21st April 1967 and passes over the private vehicular crossing which gave access to Alice Holt Forest. There was restricted sighting of the up starting – hence the banner repeater, seen in the previous photograph. Behind the train is the lamp room, adapted from a signal box that was in use from 1901 to 1905. (C.L. Caddy)

89. A double 'first'. On the first day of single line working west of Farnham (20th July 1985), the first through passenger train to the Mid-Hants Railway passed through Bentley. The Southern Electric Group chartered 6H DEMU no. 1013, normally used on Charing Cross-Hastings services. It was not the first such unit to have run to Alton as nos. 1034 and 1037 laid over in platform 3 on 28th January 1967, after working a Brighton to Aldershot football special. (C. Hall)

90. To increase operating flexibility, a passing loop was installed and came into use on 24th November 1985. 4VEP no. 7763 leaves for Alton on 12th August 1985 and passes the then inoperative down platform signal. The concrete lamp posts/hanging flower basket supports have subsequently been replaced by the red metal pattern. (J.H. Bird)

91. Security bars indicate the position of the booking office, which was still in use when photographed in June 1988. Most down trains then used the up platform, so that few passengers had to climb the footbridge. (J. Scrace)

92. When the junction details were recorded in 1957, bull head rail was standard in the area. The junction box came into use when the branch opened on 11th December 1905 and replaced two, one at each end of the station, which had been built for the doubling in 1901. (A.E. Bennett)

93. The all timber box was Bentley's fourth and was closed on 19th December 1976, when the crossover was also taken out of use. 4VEP (now class 423) no. 7705 leads the 16.56 Waterloo to Alton on 3rd June 1970. After closure, the signal box was totally dismembered for possible re-use on the Mid-Hants Railway. (J. Scrace)

London and South Western Ry.

787

TO

ALTON

KINGSLEY HALT

94. The halt was brought into use four months after the branch opened and was devoid of a shelter. A passenger arrives at the right moment, to join a push-pull set bound for Bentley. Steam railcars were used in the first years of operation. (Lens of Sutton)

The 1910 survey reveals the boundary of the land acquired for the provision of a goods yard which never materialised. The site is now occupied by houses.

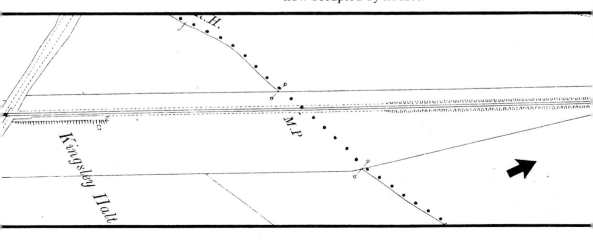

95. Class M7 no. 328 crosses the road to Binsted and begins to accelerate on the 1 in 132 falling gradient towards Bordon. Kingsley village was a ½ mile walk from the halt. (Lens of Sutton)

96. Lamps were provided at each end of the platform, these helping train crews to locate the stopping place. Another lamp could theoretically be hoisted to the top of the concrete post. Cattle grids were provided at this and the other two ungated crossings on the branch. (D. Cullum)

←

97. The 1896 Light Railways Act, under which the line was built and operated, did not require the provision of level crossing gates. Class M7 no. 30027 departs with the 10.15 am from Bentley on 9th May 1956 and fails to disturb the grazing horse. (J.H. Aston)

BORDON

98. The main buildings at the terminus of the 4½ mile long branch were steel framed, on brick surrounded bases and clad with corrugated iron sheets. The station received a lean-to extension on its east elevation in 1916. (Lens of Sutton)

The main reason for building the branch was to serve the military camps in the area and, in particular, to enable the WD to build a training railway which was known as the Woolmer Instructional Military Railway

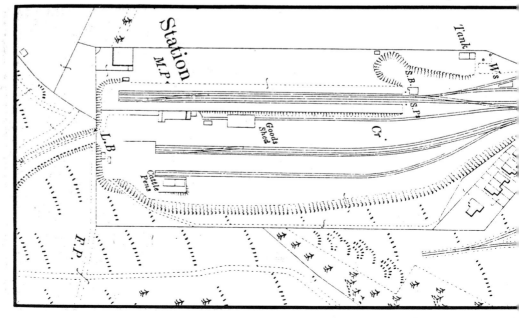

99. The sliding doors in the south end of the goods shed had been removed and the end sheeted up at an early date. The cottages in the background were built by the LSWR for their staff and still stand, although most of the site is now occupied by factories. (Lens of Sutton)

from 1908. In 1935, it was renamed the Longmoor Military Railway. The line curves away, lower right, on this 1910 map, the WIMR locomotive shed being evident.

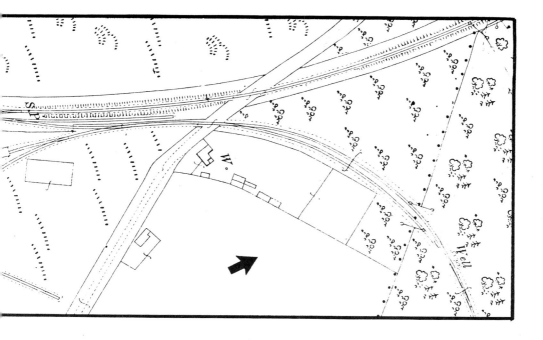

100. Gas for the station lights was originally produced in a hut next to the station, but by the time class M7 no. E128 was photographed on 17th May 1929, electricity had arrived. The up platform, on the left, was seldom used and was cut back in about 1958. The signal box had 20 levers and was officially a ground frame from 1927 until 1934 and again from 1958. (H.C. Casserley)

101. The locomotive shed, seen intact in the previous picture, was attacked by an unretarded locomotive and then left to natural forces to further the decay over many years. This is the sight in 1953, with the LMR lines on the right. By then, the branch locomotive came from Guildford each day. (D. Cullum)

102. The drab station must have added to the gloom of conscripts returning from leave. The passenger with two suitcases is passing the station master's office, there being a staff of three in the final years. Destination boards did not need changing, as the terminal platforms were on opposite sides of the train. (A.F.E. Field)

103. Between the station master's office and the main building is the former "gasworks", later used by porters and as a lamp room. The crossover was used by locomotives of goods trains, the passenger engine only negotiating it when requiring water or access to the coal stage or ash pit. (A.W. Burges)

104. U class no. 31639 stands at the terminus on 16th January 1966, with the LCGB railtour seen in picture 87 at Bentley. Generous ventilators crown the booking hall, no doubt necessary when filled with damp uniforms containing sweating soldiers. (R.E. Ruffell)

106. Regular passenger services ceased on 16th September 1957 and the last special train was operated by the RCTS on 30th April 1966, duplicating one run on the 16th. Army no. 600 2-10-0 *Gordon* also headed the last train on the LMR on 31st October 1969, the LMR platform and signal box being in the background. (R.E. Ruffell)

Other photographs and information concerning the military use of Bordon station can be found in our *Branch Lines to Longmoor*.

← 105. No. D6545 stands near the long double-sided loading platform, once used for entraining troops, horses, armaments and equipment simultaneously. The date is 28th March 1966 and the crane has a safe working load of 10 tons. Goods traffic ceased the following week, on the 4th April. (T. Wright)

107. Britain's second largest onshore oilfield was officially opened on 4th June 1986, the largest being near Swanage. It is located at Humbly Grove, three miles north of the Holybourne sidings with which it is linked by pipeline. The wells are operated by Carless and up to five trains of tankers loaded with crude oil depart each week for the Esso Refinery at Fawley. The white building in the background of this May 1986 photograph was erected during WWII as a refrigerated food store. Three sidings and a signal box (Froyle) were opened on 9th August 1942 and closed on 12th May 1970. (J.H. Bird)

ALTON

108. From 28th July 1852 until 2nd October 1865 this was the terminus of the line and is seen here in 1928, when in use as the station master's house. It was situated opposite the present station entrance and was demolished to allow for more spaces in the car park. (Late E. Wallis)

109. After the opening of the Meon Valley line to Fareham on 1st June 1903, double track was in use for one mile west to Butts Junction, but after 17th February 1935, this length was worked as two parallel single lines. Class M7 no.672 arrives with a train from Fareham on 3rd April 1937, the end of the then new and un-used conductor rail being evident. (D.H. Wakely)

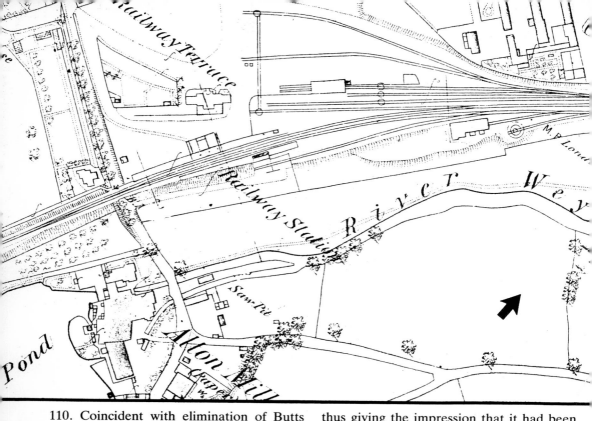

110. Coincident with elimination of Butts Junction Box was the resignalling of Alton to allow reversible running in all three platform roads. In February 1937, the platform in the foreground was extended past the signal box, thus giving the impression that it had been built adjacent to it. A Fareham train stands in platform 3, no. 2 normally being used by Winchester trains. (D. Cullum)

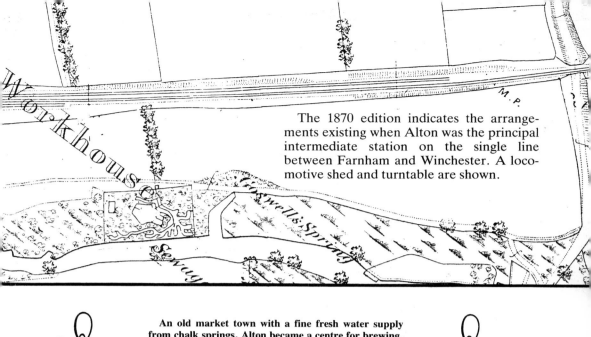

The 1870 edition indicates the arrangements existing when Alton was the principal intermediate station on the single line between Farnham and Winchester. A locomotive shed and turntable are shown.

An old market town with a fine fresh water supply from chalk springs, Alton became a centre for brewing, hops being grown over a wide area, locally. The famous Harp lager originated here and brewing continues on a large scale.

111. Beyond the bicycle shelter, in this 1969 photograph, is the corrugated iron parcels office. It was still standing in 1988 and had been acquired by the Mid-Hants Railway. DEMUs were introduced on the Alton-Southampton services in November 1959. (J. Scrace)

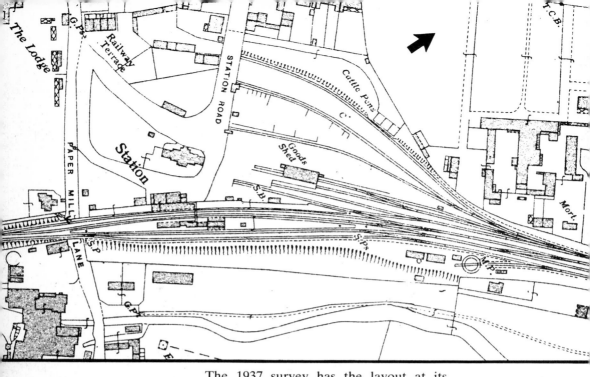

The 1937 survey has the layout at its optimum, but omits the 1935 connection from platform 2 to the Meon Valley line, which is the lower one of the two on the left.

112. A 1969 view gives an antiquated air, particularly with gas lamps in evidence. These were replaced in 1970. A welcome facelift in 1987 included non-standard paint colours, namely SR green and cream. This resulted in a "highly commended" award in a national station competition. (J. Scrace)

113. The goods yard had been beyond the fence and was closed for general freight on 6th January 1969. Platform 2 was used exclusively for the DEMUs to Southampton, the buffer stops having been put in on 9th July 1967. The signal box was closed on 28th September 1980 and was destroyed by fire shortly afterwards. (J.H. Bird)

Breweries have featured in the life of Alton for a long while. The sidings shown on the 1937 map were west of the station and branched off the Winchester line until taken out of use on 26th November 1968, when the breweries were owned by Courage & Co.

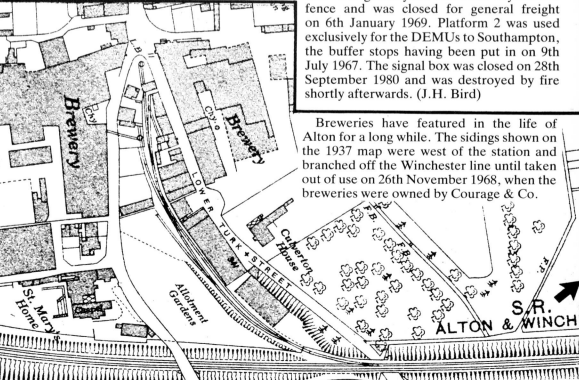

114. A view from the footbridge steps shows the 1865 shelter on platform 2 and part of the 1901 canopy on platform 3. Services to Southampton were withdrawn on 5th February 1973 and the fight to revive the line began in earnest. Some coaches were delivered by rail on 6th March 1976 and, soon after, the track between Alton and Ropley was lifted. (J.H. Bird)

115. The rear of the 10.20 to Waterloo is seen on 20th October 1973, close to the station master's office. This wooden building had been Bentley West signal box between 1901 and 1905. Conductor rail was removed from platform 3 on 28th September 1980 and relaid at platform 2, which was then reconnected at the London end. The tracks from platforms 1 and 2 then merged onto a short length of single line before joining the double track. (R.E. Ruffell)

116. On 24th July 1980, four coaches of a 12-coach arrival were detached; eight departed at 18.50 and this 4 VEP, half of which is beyond the conductor rail, waits to move forward and leave at 19.20. (R.W. Small)

117. Relaying of the Mid-Hants Railway commenced at Ropley in May 1982 and at Alton in March 1985, enabling steam services to platform 3 to start on 25th May 1985 – a remarkable achievement. On 9th January 1986, the track was removed from platform 1, in preparation for the installation of a crossover, the main use for which would be by locomotives running around empty oil tankers, bound for Holybourne sidings. No. 47286 stands with the ballast train, while no. 33033 waits on the Mid-Hants line with track panels. The old paper mill buildings, a familiar landmark on the left, were demolished in 1988.
(J.H. Bird)

Mid·hants
WATERCRESS LINE

119. The crossover is also used to release the locomotives of through trains which arrive at platform 2. This platform is also used by Mid-Hants trains on special occasions, such as pre-Christmas when Santa Specials are operated. (V. Mitchell)

118. The area leased by the Mid-Hants Railway from BR is bounded by fences between platforms 2 and 3, and one near the end of platform 1. A special train organised by the Woking Homes on 3rd October 1987 is seen returning behind no. 33101. It had been hauled from Alresford by N class no. 31874 and S15 class no. 506. The signal box was the former station master's office seen in picture 115. (J.H. Bird)

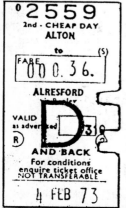

Other views of this station and of the lines to Basingstoke, Winchester and Fareham are in our *Branch Lines to Alton.*

120. Magnificently restored U class 2-6-0 no. 31806 waits to run round its train on 31st August 1987, the connecting service from Waterloo having just arrived. This rail connection gives the opportunity for travellers from London and elsewhere to enjoy a stress free journey to one of the best steam railways in Britain. (V. Mitchell)

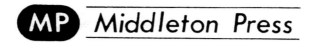

MP *Middleton Press*

Easebourne Lane, Midhurst, West Sussex, GU29 9AZ
☎ Midhurst (073 081) 3169

BRANCH LINES
BRANCH LINES TO MIDHURST
BRANCH LINES TO HORSHAM
BRANCH LINES TO EAST GRINSTEAD
BRANCH LINES TO ALTON
BRANCH LINE TO HAYLING
BRANCH LINE TO SOUTHWOLD
BRANCH LINE TO TENTERDEN
BRANCH LINES TO NEWPORT
BRANCH LINES TO TUNBRIDGE WELLS
BRANCH LINE TO SWANAGE
BRANCH LINES TO LONGMOOR
BRANCH LINES TO LYME REGIS
BRANCH LINES **AROUND** MIDHURST
BRANCH LINE TO FAIRFORD

SOUTH COAST RAILWAYS
BRIGHTON TO WORTHING
WORTHING TO CHICHESTER
CHICHESTER TO PORTSMOUTH
BRIGHTON TO EASTBOURNE
RYDE TO VENTNOR
EASTBOURNE TO HASTINGS
PORTSMOUTH TO SOUTHAMPTON
HASTINGS TO ASHFORD*
SOUTHAMPTON TO BOURNEMOUTH
ASHFORD TO DOVER
BOURNEMOUTH TO WEYMOUTH

STEAMING THROUGH
STEAMING THROUGH KENT
STEAMING THROUGH EAST HANTS
STEAMING THROUGH EAST SUSSEX
STEAMING THROUGH SURREY
STEAMING THROUGH WEST SUSSEX
STEAMING THROUGH THE
  ISLE OF WIGHT

OTHER RAILWAY BOOKS
WAR ON THE LINE
(Reprint of the SR history in World War II)
GARRAWAY FATHER AND SON
(Biography - includes LNER, Talyllyn and Festiniog Railways)

OTHER BOOKS
MIDHURST TOWN – THEN & NOW
EAST GRINSTEAD – THEN & NOW
THE MILITARY DEFENCE OF WEST SUSSEX
WEST SUSSEX WATERWAYS
SURREY WATERWAYS
BATTLE OVER PORTSMOUTH
A City at war in 1940
SUSSEX POLICE FORCES

COUNTRY RAILWAY ROUTES
BOURNEMOUTH TO EVERCREECH JUNCTION
READING TO GUILDFORD
WOKING TO ALTON

SOUTHERN MAIN LINES
WOKING TO PORTSMOUTH
HAYWARDS HEATH TO SEAFORD
EPSOM TO HORSHAM
CRAWLEY TO LITTLEHAMPTON
THREE BRIDGES TO BRIGHTON
WATERLOO TO WOKING
VICTORIA TO EAST CROYDON
TONBRIDGE TO HASTINGS
EAST CROYDON TO THREE BRIDGES
WOKING TO SOUTHAMPTON
WATERLOO TO WINDSOR
LONDON BRIDGE TO EAST CROYDON

*Video also available. Details from
M.P. Videos, 11 Park Crescent, Midhurst,
West Sussex GU29 9ED.*